# StressBusters

## TIPS TO FEEL HEALTHY, ALIVE AND ENERGIZED

### KATHERINE BUTLER, N.C.C.

## JOHN WILEY & SONS, INC.

New York · Chichester · Weinheim · Brisbane · Singapore · Toronto

This book is printed on acid-free paper. ☺

The information contained in this book is not intended to serve as a replacement for professional
medical advice. Any use of the information in this book is at the reader's discretion. The author and
the publisher specifically disclaim any and all liability arising directly or indirectly from the use or
application of any information contained in this book. A health care professional should be
consulted regarding your specific situation.

ISBN 0-471-34706-X

Printed in the United States of America

10  9  8  7  6  5  4  3  2

To my husband, Doug, who inspired the writing of this book.

# Introduction

Some people say that life is one stressful event after another, and many of us agree. But, believe it or not, we all need stress in our lives. Our mental and physical well-being depends on a certain optimal level of stress to feel healthy, alive, and energized. With too little stress, we feel bored, apathetic, and weak. Too much stress, though, and we begin to notice any number of stress symptoms listed in Section one of this book.

Because you're reading this book, chances are that you're not feeling too little stress, but—on the contrary—too much. This book will provide you with suggestions for stressbusting: those things you can do either to decrease your immediate level of stress or more effectively manage your life to eliminate unnecessary stress in the future. However, words on a page won't help you unless you act to implement some of them. First tip: Don't attempt to implement all of them, or that will cause its own stress. Each of these ideas is provided with the understanding that what works for one person may not work as well for another, so just pick those suggestions that seem most helpful to you.

A good place to start is with your stressbusting equipment, in Section two. We can't avoid many of the things in our lives that contribute to our stress. However, a great deal of stress buildup, more than we probably realize, results from inadequate care of our equipment for managing stress—our bodies and minds. If we do what we can to take care of ourselves physically and mentally, our stress hardiness increases and we are more likely to keep our stress level within the optimal range.

If your equipment is already in good shape, then you're ready to try out the stressbusting suggestions in the rest of the book. Section three focuses on ways to reduce stress related to life at home—in family relationships, finances, home management, etc. If your workplace is the source of significant stress for you, you'll want to turn to Section four and begin to practice some of the suggestions regarding dealing with conflict, managing your time, organizing your work, etc. Section five lists an additional assortment of stressbusting ideas to help you reduce or cope with stress anywhere and anytime. The last section is a collection of easy-to-do exercises to help reduce physical or mental stress symptoms and produce feelings of greater relaxation.

One final thought: Keep in mind that the goal of stressbusting is not to eliminate stress completely from your life, but only to keep it at a manageable level. Everyone will, at times, experience some of the negative symptoms of stress. When that happens, let those first symptoms serve as early warning signals. They are informing you of your need to increase your stressbusting activities, to better manage the circumstances of your life. It is my sincere hope that this book will help you to do that.

Good health and good stressbusting.

Katherine Jason Butler, M.S., N.C.C.
Chesterfield, Virginia

STRESSBUSTERS

# Signs of Stress

# Physical Stress Symptoms

| | | |
|---|---|---|
| muscle tension | frequent indigestion | frequent urination |
| dry mouth or throat | loss of appetite | increased appetite |
| chronic fatigue | insomnia | excessive sleeping |
| sexual inadequacy | excessive menstruation | menstrual distress |
| twitching nose | twitching eye | facial or jaw pains |
| difficulty swallowing | nausea and/or vomiting | intestinal distress |
| cold hands and/or feet | excessive sweating | shallow breathing |
| neck pains | backaches | headaches |
| chest pains | swollen joints | weakness |
| weight gain or loss | halting or stuttering speech | nervous tics |

| rashes or hives | dizziness | frequent colds or flu |
| ulcers on tongue | heartburn | accident proneness |
| increased allergies | pounding or racing heart | high blood pressure |
| constipation | diarrhea | ringing in the ears |
| itches for no reason | shakiness/tremors | acne breakout |

**Note:** Many of these symptoms can also be caused by serious medical conditions. Consult your doctor if any of these symptoms are intense or persistent.

# Mental and Emotional Stress Symptoms

| | |
|---|---|
| depression | moodiness |
| anxiety | anger |
| increased or unusual aggressiveness | impatience |
| feelings of panic | feelings of helplessness |
| frequent crying | irritability |
| excessive worrying | low frustration tolerance |
| decreased concentration | trouble learning new information |
| racing thoughts or disorientation | inability to make decisions |
| confused thinking | self-defeating thoughts |
| nightmares | loss of memory |

sexual inadequacy

social withdrawal

fear of losing control

emotional numbness

decreased sense of humor

restlessness

feeling overwhelmed

thoughts of suicide

Note: Consult a mental health professional if any of these symptoms are frequent or intense.

# Behavioral Stress Symptoms

gnashing or grinding teeth

increased drug or alcohol use

compulsive eating

inattention to dress or grooming

unusual behaviors

fast or mumbled speech

constant tiredness

increased number of mistakes

wrinkling forehead

foot or finger tapping

high-pitched, nervous laughter

increased smoking

decreased eating

chronic tardiness

perfectionism

sleep problems

defensiveness or suspiciousness

reduced work efficiency

overreaction to small things

repetitive body movements

hair pulling or twirling

nail biting

compulsive dieting

chronic procrastination

sudden change in social habits

constant scratching

pacing the floor

overly slow or fast body movements

YOUR STRESSBUSTING

# Equipment

A HEALTHY MIND AND A HEALTHY BODY

## Notice your early warning signs of stress and take appropriate action.

Like the dashboard warning lights in your car, your body and mind will also alert you when you're getting too close to the "red zone." Be aware of your earliest symptoms of stress (tightness in neck or shoulders, irritability, headache, anxious feeling in stomach, etc.) and make it a point to slow down, relax, and de-stress right away before the problem gets any worse. If you repeatedly ignore your stress symptoms, you may find yourself "blowing a gasket" or experiencing a total "breakdown."

## Eat well.

Avoid eating too much, too little, or too fast; avoid skipping meals. Eat a variety of healthful foods, avoiding excess sugar, salt, and fat.

Jump-start your day with a healthy breakfast.

Eating fruits and whole grains at breakfast helps provide your body with essential nutrients needed to cope with stress.

The B-vitamins in whole grains can aid concentration and help to calm anxiety.

The vitamin C in fruits helps the body restore itself from physical stresses.

## Exercise regularly.

Exercise is a good physical outlet for your body's stress hormones. It also increases energy, tones muscles, improves the cardiovascular system, and relaxes nerves.

## Get enough sleep.

Lack of sleep leads to irritability and reduced tolerance for frustration. Your mind and body de-stress from the day's activities while you sleep.

# The ABCs of Increasing Stress Hardiness

Because the body draws on reserves of B-vitamins and vitamins A and C during times of stress, it is important to eat a variety of foods containing these essential nutrients.

**Vitamin A sources:** dark green and yellow vegetables

**Vitamin B-complex sources:** whole grains, cereals, nuts and seeds, chicken, beef, dairy foods, dark green vegetables, and wheat germ

**Vitamin C sources:** fresh fruits and vegetables, such as potatoes, tomatoes, and dark green vegetables

Note: Vitamin supplements should not substitute for balanced meals. As their name implies, they are meant as supplements only, and are generally unnecessary if you eat nutritionally-balanced meals. If you choose to take supplements, educate yourself about them first. You should know, for example, that too much vitamin A can be toxic to the body.

**Eat more fiber.** Adequate dietary fiber helps to prevent gastrointestinal disorders that can be stressors in themselves. Fiber also serves to reduce blood cholesterol levels and keep the blood sugar level more constant. Foods rich in fiber include whole-grain breads and cereals, fruits, vegetables, peas, and beans. (Note: Increasing your fiber intake too quickly may also cause problems for some people, so use moderation.)

**Eat slowly and chew food thoroughly.** Gulping down food during meals can cause intestinal distress and contribute to increased feelings of tension. Taking time to chew food completely into small particles improves digestion and helps to release tension.

**Eat adequate protein to maximize the body's ability to withstand stress.** Protein, which contains essential amino acids, helps to maintain healthy functioning of the body. Healthy sources of protein include: fish, poultry (without skin), lean meat, peas, dried beans, nuts and seeds, grains, tofu, and skimmed milk products. Animal proteins should be kept to no more than 15 percent of your total diet.

## Stop chemical warfare against your body.

Caffeine, nicotine, and excess sugar produces a stress response in your body. A breakfast consisting of a cup of coffee, a cigarette, and a doughnut is guaranteed to add more stress to your day.

# Reasons to reduce or eliminate your intake of caffeine:

Caffeine dehydrates your body. Consequently, your adrenal glands, which produce stress-fighting chemicals, are hindered because they need water to function properly.

Caffeine increases anxiety, restlessness, and nervousness.

Caffeine stimulates gastric acid secretion and can cause intestinal upset.

Caffeine can cause sleep difficulties.

Caffeine sets off stress alarms within your body and can cause rebound fatigue and irritability as the effects of the caffeine wear off.

Note: To avoid the headaches that often accompany withdrawal from caffeine, taper off gradually. For example, if you drink caffeinated coffee, start with three-fourths of a cup of regular mixed with one-quarter decaf. Over a month's time, slowly increase the amount of decaf until you've eliminated all the caffeine.

## Although many people think smoking helps calm them, it actually leads to greater stress in the long run.

When the nicotine from one cigarette enters the bloodstream, the blood sugar level begins to rise, which initially feels calming. However, the blood sugar continues to rise to an unhealthy level until there is a hypoglycemic rebound effect, stressing the body and leading to feelings of tension and nervousness. When this happens, people tend to attribute their increased nervousness to causes other than the ingested nicotine and consequently reach for another cigarette, triggering another cycle of stress.

Nicotine reduces the body's supply of vitamin C, one of the stress-fighting vitamins.

Smoking interferes with the body's ability to consume oxygen, leading to shortness of breath and a reduced capacity for exercise.

Smoking increases the blood pressure and pulse rate, creating unnecessary physical stress.

Smoking contributes to cardiovascular disease, which stresses the heart. As a result, problems in circulation may develop and walking can become diffi-cult. Additional stress results from the body's inability to maintain a comfort-able body temperature, due to poor blood circulation.

## Tips for reducing the stress produced by attempting to stop smoking:

Don't try to quit when you're already feeling overwhelmed by stress.

Check out the variety of products at your local pharmacy that can help reduce the stress of nicotine withdrawal.

Watch for advertisements in your local paper or check under *Smoking* in the yellow pages for stop-smoking seminars and smoker treatment centers.

Increasing your vitamin C intake with supplements and juice helps to minimize the pain of withdrawal.

Inhaling extra air in short bursts, as if mimicking smoking, has helped many people reduce the pain of cravings.

Engage in exercise or some physical work to help the body rid itself of harmful stress chemicals caused by nicotine detoxification.

Research has shown that too much salt, sugar, and fat (especially saturated fat) in the diet can make you more susceptible to disease and less resistant to other stressors.

Rather than sugary snacks, keep plenty of fresh or canned fruits (packed without sugar) on hand.

Experiment with using more herbs and spices to flavor your food instead of salt. Try one of the commercially-prepared, natural salt-substitutes found in the spice section of your grocery store.

Limit your intake of saturated fat, such as butter and margarine. Try substituting olive oil instead.

Three 20-minute walks each week can produce health and relaxation benefits.

# 10 reasons walking is a great stress-reducing exercise.

1. Like other forms of exercise, walking helps rid your body of harmful stress chemicals.

2. Studies show overweight individuals have elevated risks of developing various chronic medical problems. A regular habit of walking will increase your metabolism and help you lose weight or at least help prevent excess weight gain.

3. Walking tones your muscles and strengthens your bones, and a strong body is less prone to various stressful injuries.

4. Your energy will increase, so you'll be able to accomplish tasks with less fatigue and better meet the challenges of daily living.

5. Walking on a regular basis can reduce your risk of heart disease, which is the number one killer of both men and women.

6. Walking for exercise has a calming effect on the brain, decreasing anxiety and elevating mood.

7. Walking is a convenient, nonpainful, nonstressful way of becoming physically fit, so you're less likely to give up on it.

8. You can walk alone, with pets, or with other people, and you can fit it into your life just about anytime, anywhere.

9. You don't have to pay to walk, so it won't stress your financial resources.

10. There's nothing to it, but to do it.

## Some suggestions for increasing your physical fitness.

Use stairs instead of escalators or elevators

Park farther from your destination

Stand, rather than sit

Walk during breaks at work

Exercise your pet

Play a sport regularly

Take a dance class

Playing while exercising produces not only physical benefits, but also psychological ones.

It not only distracts temporarily from focusing on stressful concerns, but it also leads to the release of feel-good chemicals in the brain, which can help us take a more positive approach when we return to our problems.

## Strengthen your muscles and bones to increase overall physical fitness.

Weight-bearing exercise increases endurance and energy, helps prevent excess weight gain, and reduces risk of muscle or joint injuries.

A diet rich in calcium helps build strong bones, contributing to the overall health of the body. Good sources of calcium include: dairy products, green leafy vegetables, cauliflower, broccoli, beans, and grains.

# Strengthen your body with activities such as:

walking or jogging

swimming

lifting free weights at home or at a health club

working out on exercise equipment at a health club

mowing the lawn (pushing a mower—not riding!)

bicycling

upper and lower body exercises

aerobic workouts

dancing

sports activities

Note: You should consult with your physician before starting a new program of exercise, especially if your life has been very sedentary.

## Pay attention to your posture.

Poor posture puts unnecessary stress on your body. Improving your posture will contribute to a greater flow of oxygen, proper spinal alignment, and better overall health.

# Wear appropriate shoes that fit well.

The wrong shoes for a specific activity, inadequate support, or an improper fit can cause fatigue, muscle spasms, or more serious injury to the body.

## Listen to your body.

When you're tired, take a break and rest awhile.

# A few suggestions for relaxation

breathing exercises

taking a warm bath

getting a massage

gentle stretching

dancing

listening to relaxation tapes

boating/fishing

playing music

going to a museum

riding a bike

deep muscle relaxation

walking

reading

playing games

exercising

visualization

enjoying a hobby

praying/meditating

taking a nap

swimming

in-line skating

singing

listening to music

watching a movie

gardening

playing a sport

playing with a pet

taking a vacation

drawing/painting

laughing/having fun

being with friends

watching travel videos

enjoying nature

Exercising aerobically for about 30 minutes will raise endorphin levels in the brain, which helps to soothe and calm us.

The regular practice of relaxation helps reduce blood pressure levels.

There's a strong relationship between increased exercise levels and decreased risk of coronary heart disease.

Have regular physical checkups to rule out physical causes for stress and to catch potential health problems early.

# Help yourself get a good night's sleep.

Avoid anything containing caffeine (coffee, tea, soft drinks, chocolate, etc.) for at least four hours before bedtime.

Keep physical exercise to a minimum and avoid arousing mental activity (for example, arguing or worrying about problems) for at least an hour or two before bedtime.

Limit your fluid intake for two hours before bedtime.

If you smoke, avoid smoking for at least two hours before bedtime.

Try to go to bed and wake up at approximately the same times each day.

## Trouble sleeping? Try:

taking a warm bath by candlelight, with relaxing music.

writing down all the things cluttering your mind.

drinking a warm glass of milk.

progressive deep muscle relaxation (see page 170).

counting backward from 1000.

earplugs or an eye mask to eliminate noise or light.

getting out of bed and doing something relaxing, such as reading, until you feel drowsy.

Looking for fun ways to increase your physical activity?

Check out various community activities available through recreation departments or adult education programs.

## Watch your weight.

Excess weight maximizes stress on the heart.

Keep a variety of healthful, low-calorie foods around for snacks.

Crunchy foods like apples or carrots can also help release tension in your jaw muscles.

# Decrease negative feelings by paying attention to your self-talk.

Whether you feel angry, depressed, or overwhelmed is usually a result of what *you're* telling *yourself.* Learn to catch and challenge common stress-inducing patterns of thought, such as:

Perfectionism—thinking that you or others must be perfect to be worthwhile or that a perfect performance is the only thing that matters.

"Should" statements—expecting others, and the world in general, to function according to your plan.

"Mind-reading"—assuming you know what someone else is thinking or feeling, or why they did what they did.

## Keep things in perspective.

Put your efforts toward changing what you can, then learn to accept and adjust to what you can't change.

# Avoid the tendency to blow things out of proportion.

Learn to recognize how much personal suffering you cause yourself by an overly negative interpretation of events. Make it a point to check things out and evaluate the situation thoroughly before arriving at a conclusion.

When problems arise, don't panic. Avoid engaging in useless worrying. Instead, put your energy toward devising a plan for how to handle what concerns you.

View the problem as a puzzle to solve. Have fun with it!

Gather information.

Look for resources to help you.

Generate a variety of possible solutions.

Evaluate the various possibilities.

Decide on a plan of action.

Try something else if that plan doesn't work.

## Think creatively.

If you've been trying the same thing over and over without successful results, brainstorm (alone or with others) a variety of creative alternatives. Think about coloring outside the lines, for a change!

# Learn to challenge your thinking.

Just because we think something, doesn't make it true.

Substitute stressful "what ifs…" with more realistic alternative thoughts.

Ask yourself these questions when faced with stressful thoughts:

> What evidence do I have that this thought is true?

> What evidence do I have that this thought is not true?

> Are there alternative explanations or interpretations, besides what I'm thinking? (Would someone else see it differently?)

> Is this thought part of a self-defeating pattern of thinking I've developed?

> Am I forgetting my strengths and resources?

Recognize that some of the greatest discoveries and learning experiences started out as mistakes or failures.

Rather than limiting your life by trying to avoid making mistakes, view them as opportunities for learning how you can do things differently in the future. Look for what you can learn from other people's mistakes, too. It may save you from having to make the same ones. (Always try to make *new* mistakes!)

# Rid yourself of limiting assumptions.

Consider what you may be saying to yourself that is hindering your ability to find solutions to your problems or cope more effectively. Possibilities include such self-defeating statements as:

"I can't..."

"It'll never work."

"I've always been this way."

"We've never done it that way before."

"It's too complicated/difficult/time-consuming, etc."

Don't rely on your memory—write down things you need to remember.

When faced with a problem, ask, "What can I learn from this situation?"

A difficult situation can be easier to face if you can anticipate a positive benefit coming from it.

Rather than engaging in useless worrying, put your energy toward devising a plan for how you can handle what concerns you.

Jumping to conclusions almost always leads to unnecessary stress.

When you catch yourself feeling stressed about something that may not have happened, try to consider as many alternative explanations as possible. Focus on the most realistic (not the most painful) explanation and consider this as most likely unless proven otherwise.

Watch out for wishful "if only" thinking, which can lead to discouragement and despair. Instead, ask yourself what steps you can take to better manage "what is."

Be aware of the mental trap "I can't," which tends to sap energy. Oftentimes it's more a matter of, "I am capable of doing this, but I'm not sure if I want to put forth the necessary effort." The second statement is more helpful because it leaves room for you to have a choice in the matter.

## Evaluate your expectations.

A good deal of stress comes about due to unrealistic expectations. Ask yourself if your expectations (of yourself, your life, your job, your relationships, etc.) are reasonable and achievable. If not, do what you can to make the necessary adjustments in your thinking. If you're not sure, ask others what they think.

## Reevaluate messages or beliefs you grew up with and never questioned.

Think about what you were taught (by words or actions) as a child and ask yourself if these things are really true or are they merely a reflection of someone else's idea of what is right or wrong, good or bad, or the way things should or shouldn't be. Decide for yourself which of those messages you choose to accept and which ones you can do without.

## Live in the present.

Reduce your stress by letting go of energy-draining grudges. Recognize that you keep yourself stressed by holding on to them, and this hurts you more than it does anyone else. It may help to keep in mind that you've made your share of mistakes, too.

Also, determine not to borrow trouble from the future by worrying about what might happen. Instead, use what you've learned from the past to make smart decisions today to help bring about a better tomorrow.

# Watch what you tell yourself in difficult situations.

Learn to replace self-defeating, stress-inducing thoughts with realistic affirmations, such as:

"I can stay calm and think through how to handle this."

"This isn't the end of the world. It's frustrating, but I can cope with it."

"I'm not going to spend $100 worth of energy on a $2 problem."

# STRESSBUSTING

# At Home

Do your ironing (and other stationary tasks) while you're watching TV or a rented video to make it less of a chore.

An inexpensive way to avoid running out of necessary items is to stock up on things you'll always need at home (paper towels, toothpaste, detergent, shampoo, bathroom tissue, etc.) whenever you find them on sale.

## Share the work.

Form a carpool for taking children to and from school or activities.

Delegate chores at home. Even a very young child can help clean up a room or set the table.

Join or develop a cooking co-op. Get together with several families to share cooking responsibilities for the week.

## Give yourself a break.

Do as many household chores as you can during the week so you can look forward to the weekend for fun and relaxation.

## "Keys" to stress-reduction:

Hang your keys on a holder by the door you usually enter to avoid searching around for misplaced keys.

Hide an extra house key somewhere outside in case you are locked out.

Carry an extra car key in your wallet or in a magnetized case that you attach in a hidden place under your car.

Make a duplicate set of all keys you need and keep these in a safe place.

Break large, imposing household tasks into smaller, more manageable chunks.

For example, clean out one closet or clean one room each day, rather than attempting to clean out all your closets or clean the whole house at one time.

## To avoid or reduce financial stress:

Create a budget, or revise your present one, and stick to it.

Consult a free credit counselor to help you consolidate your debts.

Read books or attend classes on how to better manage your finances.

Get financial counseling.

Cut up (or at least refuse to use) credit cards until balances are paid off.

Avoid ATM withdrawal charges by using your bank's own network. You may even want to avoid ATMs altogether if you always forget to enter your withdrawals and deposits in your checkbook, resulting in inaccurate checkbook balances.

Adjust your expectations of what you really need.

Attend or develop a parenting support group.

Cultivate intimate family relationships to help generate a sense of well-being at home.

Take time to play with your children.

Have a standing weekly date with your spouse.

Read bedtime stories to your children or spouse (or pet!) as a way to relax.

Spend more time noticing what your spouse and children do right and affirm them for that.

## Spend time with pets— your own or someone else's.

Research has demonstrated that blood pressure and heart rates drop when you hold or stroke a pet. It also reduces your breathing rate. Plus, pets are great listeners!

# Get organized.

Make a things-to-do list daily, and do the most difficult things first.

Buy a file cabinet (even a cardboard file box will do) and folders, and begin storing various papers you need or want to keep in one convenient place. Label the folders and arrange them alphabetically, so you can find what you're looking for quickly.

Keep vital items such as bills, address book, stamps, tape, tools, etc., in specially designated places to avoid the frustration of having to hunt for them.

Write down all your commitments on one calendar.

## Unclutter your life.

Look around your house and collect all the things you no longer use or need, such as: old or ill-fitting clothes, back issues of magazines, baby or children's clothes and toys, and anything in drawers, cupboards, and closets that haven't seen the light of day in months or years. Then, sell, donate, recycle, or give them away.

## Save time.

Write the same basic letter to all friends, adding some personal remarks at the end.

Cook double portions of meals, then freeze leftovers to eat later when you don't have time to fix lunch or dinner.

Use a phone answering machine to avoid being interrupted by sales calls and to screen other calls you can return at a more convenient time.

## Communicate assertively.

Learn to tell your spouse, parents, and children honestly, directly, and appropriately what you want, need, feel, and think. If this is difficult for you, read a book about assertive communication or sign up for an assertiveness class.

## Keep a journal.

Writing down thoughts and feelings in a journal can help ease mental tension and provide some clarity or direction regarding problems.

# Create your own spa.

Soak your tension away by adding therapeutic mineral salts or bubbles to the water in your bath.

Surround yourself with aromatic candles while you bathe.

Use a massaging shower head.

Buy a bathtub whirlpool insert to convert an ordinary bath into an even more relaxing one.

## Tired eyes?

Pour warm (not hot) tea into a washcloth and place it over your eyes for several minutes.

After a particularly stressful day, order take-out food and eat it by candlelight.

## Become an expert mail handler.

Sort your mail the same day you receive it. Put bills in one place, letters to answer in another, and magazines where you expect to read them. Immediately throw out mail you don't want. Find a convenient, but out-of-sight storage spot (such as an emptied-out kitchen drawer) for things you want to read (catalogs, newsletters, etc.), but that don't require immediate attention. Use any "down time" (waiting for water to boil, holding on the phone, etc.) to look at and finally dispose of what you have put away in the drawer.

## To eliminate the morning rush, plan your day the night before.

Set out the clothes you'll wear.

Make your lunch.

Think through what you need to take with you to work, and place these things near the door, or better yet, in the car.

Get up 15 to 20 minutes earlier to have time for a healthy breakfast.

## Use aromatherapy to help you relax at home.

Place scented candles, flowers, oils, or potpourri in various rooms and take time to smell them. Try putting your favorite-smelling spices in your vacuum cleaner bag to freshen the air naturally while cleaning.

Rather than losing sleep to watch a late-night TV program, use your VCR to record it to view at a more convenient time.

Plus, you can save time speeding through the commercials!

# Take control of the time you spend "on hold."

Avoid being put on hold by saying you'll call back or asking for a return call. If holding is unavoidable, choose how you want to use your time:

Read the paper or a magazine.

Sort through your drawer where you stash mail to look at later.

Attend to chores (easier with a long phone cord or a cordless phone).

Groom your pet.

Take a cat-nap.

# Cry when you feel like it.

Emotional tears help remove the buildup of stress chemicals, and people who allow themselves to cry have less of a tendency to develop stress-related illnesses.

If you need a good cry, but the tears won't come, try renting a sad movie or listening to melancholy music.

## Practice preventive maintenance.

Avoid the stress of equipment failure by keeping your car, furnace, air conditioner, major appliances, etc., in good working order.

Allow yourself and your spouse at least 30 minutes of "down" time just to relax after coming home from work.

STRESS**B**USTING

# At Work

If your job requires you to stand for long periods of time, consider wearing a light back brace over or under your clothes.

## Exercise options at work:

Bring sneakers and take a brisk walk outside around your building, or inside the building if the weather is poor.

Take the stairs, rather than the elevator, or at least get off two or three floors before yours and walk the rest of the way.

If you must sit for long periods, get up and stretch periodically (see exercises in Section six).

If your workplace has an exercise room, take advantage of it before or after work, or during breaks.

## Keep in mind Murphy's Law.

When planning how long a project will take, give yourself a little extra time
for those unforeseen interruptions or delays.

Use an appointment book and schedule in your most important activities first, then fit other activities in around those.

Make a list prioritizing what needs to be done at work, and do the most important things first.

To help get your mind off work after you leave, listen to music or books on tape during the drive home.

Stop at a gym to exercise on your way to or from work.

# Reduce computer-induced stress

Make sure your computer screen is positioned so that your head is upright in a relaxed posture and there is a very slight downward angle of your line of sight.

Sit in a comfortable chair with armrests to avoid muscle tension in your shoulders and at the base of your skull from the weight of your arms.

Use ergonomically designed wrist pads with your computer keyboard.

Lessen the strain on tense eye muscles by closing your eyes periodically for brief periods. Also, take time to look away from the screen and focus on something in the distance for a minute or two.

Reduce eye strain caused by glare by making sure you do not have a bright light or bright window behind you. You can also use a snap-on, antiglare filter over your screen.

Blink frequently to help moisten and cleanse your eyes.

If you tend to procrastinate, give yourself earlier, artificial deadlines for important projects.

Give yourself a specific reward if you finish by the artificial deadline.

Keep certain necessities at work in case of emergencies: money, panty hose, toiletries, jacket, tie, clean shirt, sweater, umbrella, etc.

## To reduce the effects of the midafternoon slump, which tends to occur between 1 and 4 p.m.:

Avoid large, heavy meals and alcohol at lunch.

Take an exercise break—get up, move around, take a brisk walk.

Eat a fruit snack.

Play some rousing music (quietly in the background) in your office.

Delegate everything you possibly can to others.

## Eliminate ambiguity.

If you're not clear about your job responsibilities or aren't sure if your performance is up to par, schedule an appointment with your boss to discuss these issues. You'll feel less stressed when you know exactly what's expected of you and have an idea of how you're doing.

# If others contribute to your stress level at work:

As much as possible, reduce your interactions with those who upset you.

Consider moving your work station if you can and if this would help.

If you are being hindered in your work, consider the pros and cons of directly confronting the issue with those involved.

Discuss your concerns with an impartial third party who may be able to advise wisely.

If you have ideas for improvements that can be made at work, either take action on them yourself or offer your suggestions to those who are in a position to take action.

Chances are your suggestions will be appreciated by others, but if your suggestion is turned down, don't take it personally. Perhaps the timing isn't right yet, or maybe your boss just isn't as perceptive as you. In either case, keep looking for ways you can make things better for yourself and others at work.

## To reduce stressful noise:

Try wearing earplugs, which you can find at most pharmacies.

Use a white noise box to mask distracting noises.

Play calming music or relaxation tapes (such as soothing sounds of nature) in the background.

Close your office door if you have one.

Dress in layers when attending seminars or conferences—or even at your own workplace—to be prepared for various temperatures.

## Make efficient use of technology.

Get broken equipment fixed.

Have outmoded machinery updated.

Keep machines from breaking down as often with regular preventive maintenance.

## Desk strategies:

Keep your work area organized to avoid confusing clutter. Use file folders and keep them alphabetized for quick access to necessary information.

On the other hand, if you can easily find what you need in the midst of what looks like a mess to others, remind yourself that your system works for you, and don't stress yourself trying to fix what isn't broken.

## Cultivate your sense of humor, even (and especially) at work.

Stock up on humorous materials (individual cartoons, cartoon books, joke books, etc.) and keep them handy. When feeling stressed, pull them out and have a good laugh.

If you can, choose a humorous screen saver for your computer.

Circulate appropriate humor materials among the office staff or post a daily or weekly cartoon in the break room.

## Set meetable, beatable deadlines when promising work for others.

You'll feel less stress if you plan for more time to finish a project than what you expect you'll need. This way you can feel good when you give your boss or client the finished work sooner than you promised. Plus, if something takes longer than expected, you've given yourself some leeway and are more likely to still meet the deadline.

## Schedule the most demanding tasks during periods of your highest energy.

Generally, it's a good idea to get your most demanding projects out of the way first.

Remind yourself to relax at work by choosing a tip from this book to use as the screen saver on your computer.

Each day choose a different tip to focus on.

**Effective lighting can relax your eyes and improve your mood and productivity.**

If possible, place your desk near a window or install full-spectrum (containing ultraviolet) fluorescent lights in your workplace.

## If you begin to rush or panic, or otherwise feel overwhelmed at work:

Stop, and focus on your breathing, gradually slowing it down until you begin to feel a sense of calmness return.

Give yourself a chance to think things through.

Ask for help.

Give yourself a relaxation break.

Break your immediate project into smaller, more manageable parts.

Stop and eat a good lunch to replenish nutrients
lost from work stress.

Make it a point to leave your desk or work station during your lunch break,
even if only for 15 to 20 minutes.

As much as possible, decide what to do with each piece of paper the first time you handle it—sign it, file it, answer now, answer later, forward it, etc.

## Plan for regular vacations from work.

Even a day or two away from work can help reduce stress and rejuvenate your spirits. A long weekend or a day off in the middle of the week can be a great stress reducer!

## Postcards for the future:

On your last day of vacation, mail a scenic postcard to yourself at work with some relaxing thoughts you'd like your "work self" to remember.

Display postcards or photos from your vacation on or near your desk to remind you to take a vacation break from it all (in your mind) for a few minutes each day.

# Do what you can to develop a sense of support and teamwork at work.

Tell others when you appreciate their efforts.

Extend support to others when you can.

Ask for support from others when you need it.

Withhold as much criticism as possible, and when not possible, communicate it in a constructive manner.

Work together to find ways to improve the general work environment.

Share, don't hoard, information.

Consult the appropriate experts in your organization for the problem you're facing (finance, personnel, marketing, engineering, etc.).

After a particularly stressful day at work, rent a no-brainer, comedy video to watch at home.

# STRESSBUSTING

# Anywhere

## Make time for play.

Do something silly, play a game, have some fun, or just act like a child. (If you've forgotten how, learn again by watching some children.) Consider play as a stress-reduction necessity, not an option.

## Put waiting time to creative use:

Bring a book, magazine, or a project to work on while waiting for a doctor or dentist appointment.

Do some relaxation exercises.

Keep some interesting reading material in your car for those times when you find yourself with unplanned excess time.

Flip through magazines while waiting in the grocery line to take your mind off the wait.

Listen to books or music on tape.

Catch up on correspondence.

## Just say no.

Practice saying no more often, or at least refrain from saying yes automatically. Instead, try saying "maybe" or "I don't know, I'll have to think about it." Take time to decide if you can spare the time and energy without adding additional stress.

## Cultivate connections with others:

Join a social activity group.

Attend adult education classes.

Get involved in volunteer work.

Become active in your church or synagogue.

## Allow more time than you think you need for whatever you're doing.

Most people underestimate how long it takes to accomplish any task. You can avoid a great deal of guilt, frustration, and stress by learning to set more realistic time limits.

## Consider joining a support group.

There are support groups available for nearly every type of need. For a listing of available resources in your community, check counseling offices, hospitals, churches, and government agencies.

## Get away to a quiet place.

Find a place you can go to periodically to be alone — to pray, meditate, get in better touch with what's going on within you, or just simply "be," rather than "do."

Be willing to ask for help when you need it.

Provide a rest for the left half of your brain by exercising the creative right half.

Make or build something.

Draw or paint.

Garden.

Cook.

Sing.

Sew.

## Exercise your sense of humor.

Laughter releases endorphins (natural pain relievers and "feel-good" chemicals) into the body.

Laughter invigorates us from within and improves blood circulation.

Being able to see the humor in a situation can help eliminate or reduce sources of tension and conflict.

Listen to tapes specifically designed to relax you:

while exercising

while engaged in an unpleasant task

while waiting for appointments

Allow at least 10 to 15 minutes extra drive time to avoid having to rush.

## Keep a "stress file."

Save articles you see in magazines or newspapers on how to manage stress, then refer to them from time to time.

Ask others what helps them to manage their stress and write down the ideas you like best.

## Inoculate yourself before facing an upcoming stressful or fearful situation.

Rehearse the event over and over in your mind, imagining every detail and how you will successfully handle it. Also, practice substituting positive (but realistic) self-statements for self-defeating negative ones. For example: "I'm beginning to feel nervous, but if I slow my breathing down and take it a step at a time, I'll be OK."

# Make time to develop satisfying close relationships.

People who report high levels of satisfaction in friendship, marriage, and spiritual support tend to be less likely to be at risk for all forms of illness and accidents.

## If you're feeling stressed, try smiling more.

There is a physical connection between the facial muscles used in smiling (whether you feel like it or not) and the part of the brain that releases "feel-good" endorphins.

## Take a proactive approach to problems you encounter.

Rather than reacting negatively, see it as an opportunity to exercise your creativity while considering a variety of possible solutions.

Anytime you conduct business on the phone, make sure you write down the name of the person you speak to and the date.

That way, if there's any problem later, you'll know whom to ask for when you call back.

When faced with a large, difficult, or otherwise imposing task, think about how you can break it down into smaller, more manageable pieces.

Ask yourself if it's really necessary to do the entire project at one time. Even if it is, you can still break it into smaller chunks, so you can stay motivated and feel a sense of accomplishment as you finish each part.

# Plan ahead for possible car emergencies or delays.

Keep a 5- or 10-dollar bill in your car at all times, in case you should find yourself low on gas with no money in your purse or wallet.

Equip your car with essential emergency items: jack, jumper cables, flare, blanket, car tool kit, first-aid kit, etc.

If you don't know how to change a flat tire, have someone teach you.

Put together a just-in-case kit of your own basic necessities, such as: an umbrella, brush and comb, some toiletry items, an extra pair of hose, headache medication, a granola bar, maps, etc.

## Avoid the quick-fix approach to stress management.

Don't rely on drugs (legal or illegal) to reduce stress. In the short term these may seem to help, but they generally make matters worse in the long run. Instead, use the suggestions in this book for healthy stress reduction.

## Give yourself a lift by boosting someone else.

Try volunteering some time at a hospital, nursing home, rehab center, or youth center. In the process of helping others you may discover that your own problems seem less significant.

## Develop realistic, meaningful goals.

Challenging, but attainable goals help keep us balanced.

Interesting and purposeful goals help keep us motivated.

## Improve your decision-making skills.

A great deal of stress can result from making poor or impulsive decisions. Major decisions, especially those concerning spouse, children, job, home, car, etc., need to be considered very carefully to reduce the possibility of long-term negative consequences. Take time in making decisions and learn to critically evaluate the pros and cons. Ask others you respect for their opinions or suggestions.

## To reduce travel stress:

Stack clothes and roll or bundle them together—they wrinkle less.

A carry-on bag with wheels saves you from lugging a heavy load around the airport.

Learn to travel light, mixing and matching your clothes so you can pack less.

If you're traveling with small children, take snacks with you as well as games or other materials to keep them occupied during the trip.

# Anticipate your gift-giving needs.

To avoid the stress of holiday shopping in December and the financial strain to your budget, try purchasing your gifts ahead of time. Anytime during the year when you happen to come across something appropriate for that special someone (maybe even on sale!), buy it, if you have the extra cash, and store it away for later. Be sure to keep a list of the people you've bought for and what you have hidden away. Then in December, when others are madly rushing about, you can just open up your closet and begin wrapping. (This also takes the stress out of buying birthday and wedding gifts.)

To avoid crowds and long lines, try to do your shopping and banking during off hours.

Learn something new just for the pure fun of it:

a sport

a line dance

a card trick

a magic trick

a new hobby

a language

an instrument

# Keep learning.

Eliminate the stress that can come from lack of information. Search out ways to improve job skills or relationships, study up on places you intend to travel, or seek help with specific problem areas. If you need or want to do something, but don't know how, try one of these sources:

libraries

bookstores

the Internet

experts in the field

friends, family members, or neighbors who have the expertise you lack

schools

community classes

# Simplify your life as much as possible.

Because stress tends to increase with complexity of life, you can ease some unnecessary pressure by:

asking yourself if all the gadgets and accessories you have to work such long hours to afford are really worth the effort.

reducing the number of magazines you subscribe to that you don't have time to read.

cutting out those activities you feel obligated to do to get ahead, but don't really enjoy.

## Clarify your values.

Think about what you want to do with your life and what is most important to you. Eliminate as many things as you can that interfere with your priorities and focus your energy on those things that are most important to you.

# Remind yourself to relax.

If you're a type-A person, who isn't used to thinking about relaxing, consider writing sticky notes to yourself and putting them in various places where you'll see them during the day—kitchen, dashboard of your car, desk, bathroom mirror, etc. Create your own messages or use some of the following suggestions:

Life is a journey, not a destination, so slow down and enjoy the ride.

Breathe in slowly through your nose and exhale slowly through your mouth.

"Picture yourself in a boat, on a river, with tangerine trees, and marmalade skies…"—the Beatles

Alternately tense and relax your muscles.

"Most men pursue pleasure with such breathless haste that they hurry past it."—Kierkegaard

Think about what you can drop from your schedule today to allow some time for yourself.

"We live too fast and coarsely, just as we eat too fast. We do not know the true savor of our food."—Henry David Thoreau

Take five. Remember, even God rested.

## Express yourself.

Relieve the tension caused by pent-up emotions by choosing among a variety of options for healthy emotional expression:

Talk about your feelings with a trusted friend, relative, God, pet, etc.

Write about your feelings in a journal, letter, poem, story, etc.

Vent your feelings through artwork, music, drama, dance, etc.

Make friends with positive, life-affirming people—those people who make you feel better just being around them.

## Let go of the myth of perfection.

Life will be less stressful if you relax your standards. Sure, this may be difficult at first, but you'll feel happier in the long run. Ask yourself what's the worst that will happen if something you're doing isn't done just right.

## For healthier, less stressful relationships, learn the art of compromise and collaboration.

In important relationships, if you win, but the other person loses, then the relationship loses...or at best, there's no net gain. Learn to work with others to achieve win-win outcomes.

## Strive for balance in your life.

Consider which areas of your life (emotional, physical, intellectual, vocational, social, and spiritual) are out of balance and seriously consider what you can do to correct them.

Let go of attempting to control other people's lives.

Recognize that the only person you have any control over is yourself, and if you focus on you, you'll find that's enough to try to manage.

# A change is as good as a rest.

A change of scenery, even for a day or two, can help you feel renewed and refreshed. Try one of the following ideas:

If you live in the city, head out to the country, or vice versa.

Go camping.

Treat yourself to a night or two at a bed and breakfast.

Be a tourist in your hometown or area. Visit some attractions close by you've never taken the time to see.

Take a day trip from your home to go shopping, fishing, sight-seeing, biking, in-line skating, picnicking, or whatever else you feel like doing.

If something isn't working right, take action: either fix it, replace it, or get rid of it.

Don't allow it to continue to aggravate you.

If you're with friends or family members at a large or crowded place, make plans for where to meet if you should get separated.

An outing will be more pleasant if you avoid the panic of trying to find a lost child or the wasted time looking for others.

# Suggestions for recharging yourself periodically throughout the day:

short walks or some other exercise

social interaction

daydreaming

listening to music

power naps

meditation

prayer

nutrition break

## To help improve your mood, put on one of your best looking outfits.

When you get up feeling a little down, this feeling can lower your confidence in your ability to manage that day's stressors. When you know you look good, you tend to feel better.

# Be good to yourself and seek out small pleasures:

Buy yourself some fresh-cut flowers.

Take time to read the book you've been wanting to read.

Sleep out under the stars.

Kick back, relax, rent a movie, and pop some popcorn.

Treat yourself to a meal at a favorite restaurant.

Take a nap in the middle of the day.

Look at your old photo albums.

## Put the worst first.

If possible, do your most unpleasant task early, so you don't have it hanging over your head all day.

## Tips for dealing with difficult, but unavoidable changes:

Consider what you've already learned from confronting other changes in your life.

Identify and focus on all possible positive aspects of the change. For example, view the change as an opportunity for personal growth and development.

Take stock of what resources (social support, life skills, problem solving ability, intelligence, material resources, etc.) you have to help you make the best of the new situation.

Learning about common gender differences can minimize stress and conflict due to lack of understanding of the opposite sex.

Check your public library or favorite bookstore for books on this subject. Two helpful books to start with are, *You Just Don't Understand,* by Deborah Tannen, and *Men Are From Mars, Women Are From Venus,* by John Gray.

When taking long car trips, try listening to books on tape to make the drive more enjoyable and the time seem to pass more quickly.

Remember the two classic rules of stress management:

1. Don't sweat the small stuff.

2. It's all small stuff.

# STRESSBUSTING

# Exercises

## "Four Fours" Deep Breathing

Slowly inhale through your nose for 4 counts, then slowly exhale through your mouth for 4 counts. Do this for at least 4 minutes, 4 times each day for less stress and greater relaxation.

Note: To make sure you are breathing properly, place one hand on your abdomen. You should feel your abdomen expand slightly as you inhale and contract as you exhale.

# Progressive Deep Muscle Relaxation

Starting at your head, tense one of the muscle groups (eyes, jaw, tongue, fore-head) around your face for 5 to 7 seconds each, then immediately let go of the tension. Relax as completely as you can for about 30 seconds before going on to a new muscle group. When you finish with your head, repeat this same tightening–relaxing process for the other muscle groups of your body—neck, shoulders, arms, back, stomach, buttocks, legs, feet. It will take approximately 20 to 30 minutes to relax your entire body, and when you're through —if you've done it properly—you should feel like a bowl of jello.

# Mind Vacation

Sit quietly, close your eyes, and picture yourself in a peaceful setting. It could be somewhere you've been before (a cabin in the woods) or somewhere you've only dreamed of (your own private island!). Try to imagine it as vividly as possible, getting all your senses involved—what are you seeing (ocean, mountains, inside setting, etc.), feeling (breeze, warmth of sun, comfortable chair, etc.), hearing (birds, waves, rustle of leaves, etc.), and smelling (flowers, pines, salt air, etc.)? Allow yourself at least five minutes to experience the sensations and the relaxation you feel in the imagined surroundings. After you've taken the time to enjoy the peace and calm, slowly stretch and open your eyes. Remember you can go back to visit anytime, and you don't even need a Visa card!

## The Giraffe Stretch

While standing, slowly breathe in while raising your right arm straight above your head. Keeping your arm raised, slowly breathe out. As you breathe slowly in again, stretch your arm as if it were a giraffe's neck trying to reach a leaf on a tall tree. Breathe out slowly and gradually lower your arm back down to your side. Repeat with your left arm, and then with both arms together.

## The Elephant Sway

While standing with feet shoulder-width apart and with knees slightly bent, begin to curl forward while bending from the waist. Bend over as far as is comfortable for you without straining. Allow your arms to just hang down naturally in front of you. Very gently, sway from side to side, shifting your weight from foot to foot. Don't forget to breathe slowly throughout the exercise. (And while you're at it, be on the lookout for any peanuts on the floor.)

## Shoulder Roll

While breathing slowly in and out, draw your shoulders up toward your ears and move them forward in a circle. Repeat 5 to 7 times. Now begin rolling your shoulders in backward circles for 5 to 7 rotations.

## Neck Stretch

Reach your right arm behind your back and grab your wrist with your left hand. Slowly drop your left ear toward your shoulder, while at the same time pulling your right arm farther to the left until you can feel the stretch in your neck muscles. Hold this for about 20 seconds while slowly moving your chin into different positions to ease various spots of tension in your neck. Repeat the exercise with your left hand behind your back and your right ear dropped toward your shoulder.

## Head Rotation

Slowly turn your head to the right as far as possible. Hold that position for the count of 10. Return to face forward, then repeat to the left. Do each side several times.

## Torso Rotation

Standing with feet shoulder-width apart and hands on hips, rotate (twist) your torso as far to the right as you can and hold for 5 seconds. Return to face front, then rotate to the left and hold for 5 seconds. Repeat both sides 5 times.

## Hand Stretch

Curl both hands into fists and hold tight for 7 seconds. Release fists and spread fingers wide apart. Hold for 5 seconds. Repeat 3 times. Try to do this at least once an hour when you're working on a keyboard.

# Back and Leg Relief

With your back flat on the floor, bend your legs upward at the hips and make a right angle with your knees to rest your lower legs on a couch in front of you. You will look as if you are sitting in a chair that has fallen backwards. (If you're in your office, you'll probably want to close the door!) Allow yourself to simply rest in this position for 5 to 10 minutes. Pillows can also be piled up under your legs to achieve a "sitting" position if a couch is not available.

## Ankle Roll

Lifting your right leg off the ground, bend your right foot at the ankle and roll in circles to the right 5 times. Change directions and roll to the left 5 times. Repeat the exercise with your left ankle.

# Dear reader,

I truly hope that many of the tips in this book have helped you to reduce or better manage your stress. Obviously, though, there are many more ideas for stress reduction than those suggested in this book. If you have a favorite stress-reduction strategy to share for possible future editions of this book, please write it down and send it to me. I would enjoy sharing your idea with others. Thank you, and keep StressBusting!

Katherine Jason Butler
StressBusters
P.O. Box 2942
Chesterfield, VA 23832